DATE DUE

PRINTED IN U.S.A.

ALL ABOUT DINOSAURS

DIPLODOCUS

by
Amy Allatson

KidHaven
PUBLISHING

PHOTO CREDITS

Abbreviations: l-left, r-right, b-bottom, t-top, c-center, m-middle

3 - boscorelli. 4–5 - Linda Bucklin. 6-7 boscorelli. 8-9 background - Alexandra Lande. 8br - Philll. 8m - 2j architecture. 9ml - Phill. 9bl - Fresnel. 9br - Catmando. 10 background - JaySi. 10br - Catmando. 11 background - Catmando. 12 background - Catmando. 13 background - Catmando. 13br - aleksandr hunta. 13br - CoolKengzz. 14 background - Aleksandr Bryliaev. 15 background - Catmando. 16 backgorund - Elenarts. 17 background - Elenarts. 18ml - MarcelClemens. 18br - guysal. 18-19 background - Iakov Kalinin. 19m - Marques. 20-21m - Linda Bucklin. Images are courtesy of Shutterstock.com, with thanks to Getty Images, Thinkstock Photo, and iStockphoto.

Published in 2018 by
KidHaven Publishing, an Imprint of Greenhaven Publishing, LLC
353 3rd Avenue
Suite 255
New York, NY 10010

© 2018 Booklife Publishing
This edition is published by arrangement with Booklife Publishing.

Designer: Natalie Carr
Editor: Charlie Ogden

Cataloging-in-Publication Data

Names: Allatson, Amy.
Title: Diplodocus / Amy Allatson.
Description: New York : KidHaven Publishing, 2018. | Series: All about dinosaurs | Includes index.
Identifiers: ISBN 9781534521773 (pbk.) | ISBN 9781534521735 (library bound) | ISBN 9781534521650 (6 pack) | ISBN 9781534521698 (ebook)
Subjects: LCSH: Diplodocus–Juvenile literature. | Dinosaurs–Juvenile literature.
Classification: LCC QE862.S3 A45 2018 | DDC 567.913–dc23

Printed in the United States of America

CPSIA compliance information: Batch #BS17KL: For further information contact Greenhaven Publishing LLC, New York, New York at 1-844-317-7404.

Please visit our website, www.greenhavenpublishing.com. For a free color catalog of all our high-quality books, call toll free 1-844-317-7404 or fax 1-844-317-7405.

CONTENTS

Words that appear like this can be found in the glossary on page 23.

WHAT WERE DINOSAURS?

Dinosaurs were **reptiles** that lived on Earth for more than 160 million years before they became **extinct**.

There were many different types of dinosaurs. They lived both on land and in water—and some could even fly!

WHEN WERE DINOSAURS ALIVE?

Dinosaurs first lived around 230 million years ago during a time called the **Mesozoic** Era. The last dinosaurs became extinct around 65 million years ago.

All land on Earth was together in one piece during the time of the dinosaurs. Over time, it has slowly split up into different continents.

WHEN ALL THE LAND ON EARTH WAS TOGETHER IN ONE PIECE IT WAS CALLED PANGEA.

EURASIA

NORTH AMERICA

SOUTH AMERICA

AFRICA

ANTARCTICA

PANGEA

DIPLODOCUS

NAME	*Diplodocus* (duh-PLAH-duh-kuhs)
LENGTH	90 feet (27.4 m)
WEIGHT	20 tons (18 mt)
FOOD	herbivore
WHEN IT LIVED	145 million–160 million years ago
HOW IT MOVED	walked on four legs

Diplodocus was one of the biggest dinosaurs ever to live on land. It was a member of a plant-eating family of dinosaurs called sauropods.

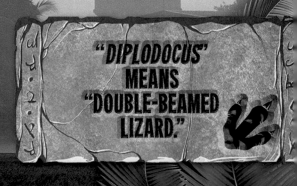

"DIPLODOCUS" MEANS "DOUBLE-BEAMED LIZARD."

Diplodocus lived 145 million to 160 million years ago. Then, it became extinct. It lived around the same time as *Stegosaurus* (steh-guh-SOHR-uhs).

STEGOSAURUS HAD FOUR SPIKES ON ITS TAIL TO PROTECT ITSELF.

DIPLODOCUS

STEGOSAURUS

WHAT DID *DIPLODOCUS* LOOK LIKE?

Diplodocus was a very long dinosaur with a tail that was 46 feet (14 m) long. It had a small head and a large body.

DIPLODOCUS USED ITS LONG TAIL TO PROTECT ITSELF FROM OTHER DINOSAURS.

Diplodocus also had a very long neck. It used its neck to reach the leaves growing on tall trees and to reach the ground to drink water.

WHERE DID DIPLODOCUS LIVE?

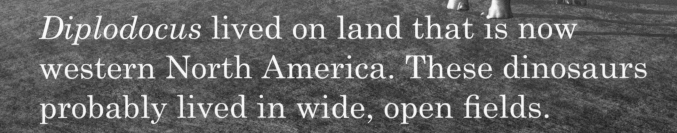

Diplodocus lived on land that is now western North America. These dinosaurs probably lived in wide, open fields.

Diplodocuses lived in **herds**. We know this because many of their **fossils** have been found together. They also traveled together to look for food, just as elephants do today.

TRAVELING IN HERDS WAS NOT THE ONLY THING *DIPLODOCUSES* HAD IN COMMON WITH ELEPHANTS—THEIR FEET WERE ALSO VERY SIMILAR.

WHAT DID DIPLODOCUS EAT?

Diplodocus was a herbivore. Its diet was made up of plants and plant parts, such as the leaves found on trees. We know this by the shape of its teeth, which scientists believe were used to grind plants.

Rocks and stones have also been found inside *Diplodocus* stomachs. They swallowed these to help them **digest** the plants they ate.

REPTILES, SUCH AS CROCODILES AND ALLIGATORS, ALSO SWALLOW STONES TO HELP THEM DIGEST THEIR FOOD.

WAS *DIPLODOCUS* THE BIGGEST PLANT EATER?

BRACHIOSAURUS

Diplodocus was one of the longest plant-eating dinosaurs at 90 feet (27.4 m) long. *Brachiosaurus* (brah-kee-oh-SOHR-uhs) was close to this length at 82 feet (25 m).

The biggest plant-eating dinosaur that we know of was *Argentinosaurus* (aar-juhn-tee-nuh-SOHR-uhs), which could reach a length of 115 feet (35 m) and a weight of 100 tons (91 mt).

ARGENTINOSAURUS

ARGENTINOSAURUS WAS 21 TIMES LONGER THAN AN AVERAGE HUMAN'S HEIGHT.

HOW DO WE KNOW...?

We know so much about dinosaurs thanks to the scientists, called paleontologists, who study them. They dig up fossils of dinosaurs to find out more about them.

FOSSIL

EGG

Scientists put together the bones they find to try to make the full skeletons of dinosaurs. From these skeletons, scientists can often figure out the size and weight of a dinosaur. We can also find out information about what it ate from its fossilized food and waste.

SKELETON

SCIENTISTS EVEN FIND FOSSILIZED EGGS AND FOOTPRINTS BELONGING TO DINOSAURS.

FACTS ABOUT DIPLODOCUS

LONG AND POWERFUL TAIL

ITS BACK LEGS WERE BIGGER AND STRONGER THAN ITS FRONT LEGS, WHICH MEANT IT COULD STAND ON ITS BACK LEGS TO REACH FOOD.

90 FEET (27.4 M) LONG

SMALL HEAD

LONG NECK FOR REACHING FOOD AND WATER

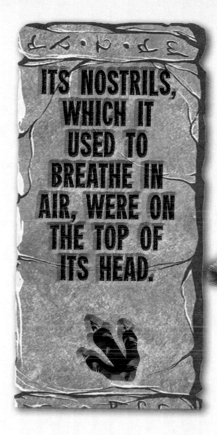

ITS NOSTRILS, WHICH IT USED TO BREATHE IN AIR, WERE ON THE TOP OF ITS HEAD.

IT WEIGHED TWICE THE AMOUNT OF A *TYRANNOSAURUS REX.*

DRAW YOUR OWN DINOSAUR

THINK ABOUT THESE QUESTIONS . . .

1. How does it move?

2. Does it live on land or in water?

3. What does it eat?

4. What color is it?

5. How big is it?

GLOSSARY

continents one of the seven great masses of land on Earth

digest to break down food in the stomach

extinct to no longer be alive

fossils the remains of plants and animals that lived a long time ago

herbivore a plant-eating animal

herds groups of animals that live together

Mesozoic a period of time when dinosaurs lived from 252.2 million years ago to 66 million years ago

reptiles cold-blooded animals with scales

INDEX